AT HOME

Dior / Lindbergh / Ar

Dior / Lindbergh / Ne

AT HOME

EVOCATIVE AND ART-FORWARD INTERIORS

BRIAN PAQUETTE

PHOTOGRAPHS BY HARIS KENJAR

GIBBS SMITH
TO ENRICH AND INSPIRE HUMANKIND

First Edition
25 24 23 22   5

Text © 2021 Brian Paquette
Photographs © 2021 Haris Kenjar
except page 160 © Jenny Jimenez

Published by
Gibbs Smith
P.O. Box 667
Layton, Utah 84041

1.800.835.4993 orders
www.gibbs-smith.com

Designed by Sheryl Dickert
Printed and bound in China

Gibbs Smith books are printed on either recycled, 100% post-consumer
waste, FSC-certified papers or on paper produced from sustainable
PEFC-certified forest/controlled wood source. Learn more at www.
pefc.org.

Library of Congress Cataloging-in-Publication Data

Names: Paquette, Brian, author. | Kenjar, Haris, photographer.
   Title: At home : evocative & art-forward interiors / Brian Paquette ;
photographs by Haris Kenjar.
   Description: First edition. | Layton, Utah : Gibbs Smith, 2021.
   Summary: "Evoking memories of the past and aspirations for
the future to create unique contemporary interiors." --Provided by
publisher.
   Identifiers: LCCN 2020030934 | ISBN 9781423654186 (hardcover)
| ISBN 9781423654193 (epub) Subjects: LCSH: Paquette, Brian--
Themes, motives. | Interior decorators. | Interior decoration.
   Classification: LCC NK2004.3.P364 A2 2001 | DDC 747--dc3
   LC record available at https://lccn.loc.gov/2020030934

TABLE OF CONTENTS

ACKNOWLEDGMENTS

In writing these acknowledgments, it is not lost on me how immensely grateful I am to be able to write a book in the first place. I had dreamt about it, of course, after countless years of flipping through monographs of the artists, designers, architects, and creatives whom I look up to.

This book is for anyone who has a dream or vision for how they want to live and be in this life. This book is for anyone who has carved their own path out of a desire to change the norm. This book is for anyone who has been told no, over and over again, yet still persisted. This book is for you.

None of this would be possible without the immense support of my family and friends, in work and in life: My team over the years, LC, SD, BK, LC, LG, MG, PS, and BW—you added your own voice to every aspect of what you did, you challenged me, and you were on the ride wherever it took us.

Katie, and everyone, at Gibbs Smith—for believing in my work enough to publish this book you are holding. Without your faith in me this would not be possible.

My family, Mom, Dad, Michelle, and Sean—you have always been my cheerleaders. My clients, who took a risk on a kid who figured things out as he went but never took your support for granted—without your trust and patronage this book would not exist. My friends and chosen family who continue to support me and my dreams—you are there with laughs, food, songs, movies, inspiration, and always make me want to be a better person through your example.

All of our vendors and collaborators who design and make beautiful things that fill our clients' homes—we treasure this family of small businesses who are engaged and want to push themselves creatively as much as we want to.

Grant—you have been a mentor and brother to me from the beginning. Thanks for taking that first invitation. Kate, my ride or die—thanks for always being there.

This book is dedicated to my loving husband, Justin, and our dogs, George and Oliver. Our small but mighty family is what means the most to me.

INTRODUCTION

I felt all at once cheated and mystified the first time I viewed a Joan Miró painting in person. As art students, we had been sold on the textbook idea that a Miró painting consisted of simple composition, perfectly drawn lines, and out-of-the-tube primary colors. But this simplification couldn't be further from actuality. His paintings are covered in the human hand and touch: guide lines, muddy colors, and paint that appears to have been mixed on the canvas itself, opposed to on the safety of a painter's palette. The paint, cracked and yellowed with age, causes the canvas to become an entirely new surface in and of itself. This heightened visual and textural experience during a college field trip to Yale University Museum speaks volumes on how I think about home and space. As an interior designer, I have set out to create homes that embrace this kind of patina, that look forward to the aging process while remaining wholly present in their comfort and setting.

I find it limiting to talk about any one approach when asked about my "style" or "look" (a question I equally love and loathe). This is mainly due to my lack of interest in any one particular style. My work has always been about reference and sense memory. It is my duty to conjure the reference and sense memories of those who inhabit the spaces we are working on. What is the past like for them? What is their lifestyle goal? What are their hopes and dreams, and what has brought them to this particular time and place?

Reference is an interesting term and I'll break it down as such: If you think of your life as a book, what are the chapters? Who are the key players? What are the elements, behaviors, good (and bad) memories, etc. that make you who you are?

In my work we must dissect these influences to make sure each new client's home references all that embodies them as individuals; their home should serve as a reference to what supports and comforts them. For example: Is there something special about where you grew up? I, myself, grew up surrounded by beaches and water. I can't seem to get quite comfortable if I'm not in that environment, but seaside living may not always be an option. So how, as a designer, do I interpret the sea, and the memories that surround it, into my home without just slapping a giant painting of waves above the sofa? How are these memories translated in a way that spark the senses without hitting you over the head? This thoughtful reflection is where we begin.

Sense memory is another major theme in my work. Perhaps it's a smell that brings you back to a positive memory. I recall my mother telling me her favorite smell is the scent of burning leaves. As a child, she would ask my grandmother to circle the neighborhoods where people were burning leaves in the fall—my mother would ride with her head out the car window, perfectly engulfed with this scent that just made her happy. There is a shade of blue I refer to as 10,000-leagues-under-the-sea blue. It reminds me of seeing the plein air painters on the beach when I was young; it reminds me of the velvet drapes in my grade school's auditorium before a recital; it reminds me of floating in the sea as a little kid, and even now, as an adult, of floating in the sea while on vacation in Hawaii. This color moves me—it's unstoppable. How do we keep your memories alive in your home—a place that should embody all that is you? Is it in the fabric? Is it in the placement of furniture for light exposure? Is it in the surface texture? It's all of these things and more, and it's how I build rooms.

The timeline of my creative path is like many others'—nonlinear. I was born and raised in Rhode Island, the adopted son of two type-A, very smart and driven parents who both worked in the medical field. I came into this world with a paintbrush in my hand, a voice to be heard, and swish in my step. I also, like many, never fit into any sort of mold I may have been pushed toward. When I was six years old, I built a stage in my basement to perform musicals I had adapted from my favorite movies at the time or just to sing my little lungs out. Scissors, tape, needle, and thread to make alterations to things in the house were off limits to me after the age of ten. I was, for the most part, content to keep myself occupied and was never one to excel at team sports or group activities. I loved my room and all the possibilities in my brain. I was lucky enough to attend great preparatory schools, but I struggled to no end with the day-to-day assignments and socialization. I did, however, excel in art class where I was encouraged to draw outside the lines for forty-five minutes

a day, two days a week. Try as they may, my parents would have little to no luck steering me toward a practical future in school.

In high school I mostly kept to myself, not always by choice, but by then I had become too used to this quiet life full of secluded introspection to change. I played music, excelled in art, and neglected the rest of my assignments. As a teenager, I also discovered punk rock. This would become a very big part of the next chapter in my life. Finding a group of other wallflowers and creatives made me feel comfortable in social settings for the first time in my life. Punk rock is always about the disenchanted or ignored coming together, exploring a new way, and not feeling so left out. During this time, the friends I made, the art I created, the bands I played in, and the new lifestyle I had discovered clashed severely with my upbringing. This juxtaposition would become the foundation for my life as a creative, still serving me to this day.

I graduated college with a degree in fine arts with a focus on conceptual art—mainly doing large-scale installation pieces involving painting, printmaking, photography, and space. I was heavily influenced by artists such as Barry McGee, Brice Marden, Uta Barth, Matthew Barney, Ida Applebroog, and Louise Bourgeois (to name a few), and I excelled in college due to my ambition and my need to push things just a bit further beyond the canvas, so to speak. During those years I kept mostly to myself, socially, but the work I was creating was defiant and prolific in scale—often surprising my peers and instructors who may have written me off.

After college I struggled to maintain a studio practice and a job at the same time. In school, art was pretty much all I needed to focus on, but, out of school, I had to support myself too. I saw this dilemma as black and white: I couldn't work a day job and also be a prolific artist. I found work at an art gallery in a summer town, which was quite isolating once the

This home's neutral but textural palette was dreamt up to let the eye travel naturally and to allow the broad art collection to sing. Curved lines and soft surfaces balance the hard lines of the architecture.

weather cooled and the vacation crowds left. It gave me a lot of time to think.

Through the gallery, I met an interior decorator by the name of John Peixinho (the go-to designer for the old-money, WASPy elite in our town) while assisting him with art purchases and framing of vintage ephemera. John saw potential in me—an eye for scale and color and a polishable demeanor that could stand up to the clientele he worked for—so he hired me to project manage at his firm. I was immediately in over

my head but enthralled by the interior design business and industry. The textiles, the antiques, the homes . . . these were the homes hidden behind the tallest hedges (growing up a middle-class kid in a very wealthy area had never before granted me any invitations). I was excited by the history of the homes we worked on, the design process, and the beautiful interiors John's firm created—and I wanted this career for myself.

While working for John, I slowly got back into painting. Another pivotal figure in my life, the artist

Jeremy Miranda, was a talented and prolific landscape painter from my hometown. The gallery I worked for represented him and we became friends. We began plein air painting together in the early mornings and evenings all over the island, learning about each other, art, and having a blast. Jeremy was just in Rhode Island for the summer; he and his soon-to-be wife lived in Portland, Oregon, where they both had studio practices and had discovered the holy grail of cool at the time. I visited them that fall and fell in love with the

Sculptural forms, antiques, and a sense of calm were the directives in this home. While its inhabitants love minimalist design, they also wanted the home to feel warm during the colder months. Cushions for either side of the fireplace and easily movable ottomans make for extra seating and visual interest.

idea of living as an artist in Portland; I made it my mission to move to Oregon by the following summer and so it was. I sold everything I owned and, against my mother's wishes, headed out into the unknown (without a job) to become a painter again. Portland had other plans for me.

I arrived with all the hopes and dreams of living an artist's bohemian life: riding bikes, hanging out in parks, meeting people with exciting and new ideas . . . I was 3,500 miles away from anything I knew and, for the first time in my life, I felt a freedom to be who I was meant to be—or at least the freedom to blossom clumsily into that person over the next few years. I had some savings, so I wasn't looking for a job immediately. I wanted to paint and paint I would—but what would I paint? What did I have to say? I began dozens of paintings, but I never actually finished a single work while in Portland. I craved the structure of school and felt too overwhelmed with all

the things I wanted to explore to sit down and produce thoughtful work—and so I didn't. When the time came for me to find a job, I started out as a sample librarian at a textile and furniture showroom. There I drowned myself in all of the lines they represented: Glant Textiles, Clarence House, Larsen . . . these names have followed me ever since. It was a menial job, but I did everything I could to elevate it. I would take the new collections I thought certain designers would like to their offices on my bike; I rearranged the showroom countless times; and I paid my dues with all the seemingly boring tasks. In my off-hours I helped friends design their places and I read every design-related book and magazine article I could get my hands on. I was obsessed. I knew a career in interior design was what I wanted. I just needed to keep my head down and work for it.

Then the recession hit. The financial crisis of 2008 was a disaster for everyone and I lost my job at the

OPPOSITE AND ABOVE: Colors such as sap green, umber, walnut, gray, ochre, and ocean blue reflect the outdoors, making the home feel even bigger.

showroom as a result. I felt like a hobo: completely lost and untethered—as if I could jump a train to anywhere and just see what happened. I applied to jobs all over the country, though hopelessly assumed I would just end up moving into my parents' basement back in Rhode Island. But with a stroke of luck, someone in Seattle took a chance on me and hired me to manage a high-end furniture showroom. I moved to Seattle without knowing a single person or having a place to live, and with barely two nickels to rub together. I figured it out as I went with the help of a couple new friends who offered up some furnishings and a landlord who, for some reason, allowed me to take an apartment with no deposit and my promise to make up the rent two months after I moved in. Getting settled in Seattle was tough. It was lonely but I felt a new kind of freedom there: a fresh start in a new city that knew nothing about me. I started a blog called BP Interiors then as well. It was simply a visual collection of ten images posted each day, which I gathered from various online sources. As I blogged, I met other designers from all over the world who were also blogging, and it opened my eyes to many diverse voices in the industry.

One day, a young couple came into the Seattle showroom and we struck up a conversation. They were shopping to furnish their first home, a condo in the Capitol Hill neighborhood of Seattle. We shared a common design language and a few weeks later they hired me for what would be my first real decoration job. I scrambled to assemble a team of workrooms and tradespeople in the area to make it happen. Over the next year we completed the home and that allowed me to quit my existing job at the showroom and start interior decorating full time. Looking back, I realize this was a silly move: quitting my job as the only other job I had was coming to an end? But also in hindsight, I firmly believe I needed that kick in the butt to get going and make this career happen for myself.

Over the next few years I helped friends in their homes and a few clients on small-scale projects, while also working part-time in marketing for a men's fashion company to help make ends meet. Fast and loose was my motto back then and, to be honest, it kind of still is. Over ten years I have grown the company to include as many as eight employees at one time, a store, multiple office locations, show houses, product lines, magazine shoots, and projects in different states and countries. It wasn't always easy, and not every venture has been successful, but I believe each step was what I was supposed to be doing at the time, and those steps have led me here.

At the time of writing this introduction, it's been more than a year since I closed the store and scaled the business back to include just myself and one other person. This decision was one of the best I have ever made. Life and love became paramount to me about three years ago when I met my now-husband, Justin. All the work and time and endless days didn't seem to matter as much to me anymore. What matters is life, love, and a continuation of the creative conversation: to be intentional with the work I do, to be thoughtful to the environment around me, to allow for space to breathe and think and be, and to be inspired. To listen when I need to hear a new voice that may direct the next chapter. Homes have been the product of my creativity for the past ten or so years and it may continue that way for the next ten, but it also may not. The important thing is to connect with your paintbrush, whatever your paintbrush may be. Connect with your environment, connect with the people around you, and add a little when it seems right.

OPPOSITE: I love when there is room to do upholstered seating and banquettes in kitchens. These elements help soften a space that is often only inhabited by hard materials.

PROCESS

The process of interior design can take many paths—I imagine it is different for each and every designer. For me, the whole process is less of a scheduled event with start and end dates, and more of a lifetime affliction: my eyes never stop observing and my brain constantly collects ideas from all types of sources.

Source material, the good stuff, isn't found in a material library or in a showroom. It is the arresting emotional pull that comes from a weekend away from the city; it is a walk during golden hour; it's the lapel of a woman's shirt seen at lunch—it is the in-between. It is not something that only occurs during 9–5, and that can be hard for some to grasp.

When I was first starting out, I felt an immense pressure to pull inspiration from every source surrounding me and beyond. I was being so literal about reference and inspiration. I thought everything needed to be a reflection of that very moment and I would hang on every word from the client or the objective. If the client liked blue-and-white china, I thought I needed to install a wall of blue-and-white china instead of, say, use those colors throughout the space in multiple tones, then choose to put one beautiful piece of china on display. This approach left little room for experimentation and it put inspiration on a schedule. That's just not how it's meant to be.

Once it had sunk in that designing peoples' homes was my actual job, and that for me to be successful it would require constant movement and the gathering of ideas (in lieu of waiting for a specific project before beginning the process), I found my work to be more impactful. It also required a talented team to make sure the rest of the process, whether that be budgeting or management, went off with as few hiccups as humanly possible.

At the beginning of my career, in those first years of errand running and administrative work, I worried that I wasn't following the creative journey I was meant for. I thought I was supposed to be a painter in the woods, living a quiet life with few outside sources. I now know enough about myself to know that would have lasted a week. I need the juxtaposition of energies. I need the quiet, the bustling, and the many sources of a city to create what truly satisfies me.

Once I realized that my strength was in sight, interpretation, and project vision, and that I could spend countless hours being and doing (and yes, of course, having client meetings and running the day-to-day of a business), I felt free and almost satisfied with the work in front of me. I say *almost* satisfied because this is a constant struggle. Along with the freedom to see and be, and have that be my strength and mission, I am constantly aware of this desire to see all that I can, and aware of all the things I might be missing. I hone in on every image, every art opening, every little side street

while walking . . . it's an okay problem to have, but still, one that I remain very mindful of.

These observations (these objects, these feelings, these colors), they all strike a chord. The goal, to me, is that they hit multiple senses—that's the true test. Can you see a shade of ochre on a chair and not only think of autumn leaves from your childhood, but also smell the air in October and hear a song that brings you right back to that moment? Cataloging these moments can be a bit clumsy and all too often it is done on my phone, either through the camera or in notes. I often think of this digital cataloguing part as a distraction to the real, palatable beauty that is happening at the time but, hey, it works.

I work with clients to get to the root of the intention, function, and aesthetic they are after in those first few meetings. Most of the time I do not know these people very well yet and so, rightfully, we all have our guard up at the beginning. I do my best to decipher, for instance, what comfort means to them or what a certain color means to them. It's a dance of making my clients feel comfortable in the process and also challenging them to give me as much of themselves in those moments we have together so that I can do my best job. Honesty is paramount in this process. I want to know what clothing they choose to put on their bodies, not what color they would choose for a chair. I want to know what time they go to bed and wake up and what they do in the hours in between. I want to know where they have traveled and where they have felt a pull to stay longer. If they work, I want to know what drives them to do so. I want to know their past just as much as their idealized future. How do they entertain and what does that mean to them? What artists', creatives', musicians', or designers' work do they connect with and why? I don't simply supply my clients with a questionnaire, which would feel too much like an assignment—like something you would give someone who is applying to school or buying a car. While interior design is a business, my process is not transactional. I prefer to treat this introductory time with my clients like dating, where we share the ideas pooling out of our heads to get to some greater truth—a creative conversation. For me, I cannot do my job without this creative exchange, and have turned down projects where a client is too busy to engage in this way. There must be a million interior designers in the world, maybe more. Find someone whom you would let run wild in your space without hesitation, and find someone with whom you'd want to hang out. This is a personal process; it is not fast, nor easy, nor inexpensive. Know that the person you have hired has your back and that you have theirs as well.

My process, after these conversations regarding reference and sense memory, is a bit more formulaic. We are building spaces after all, and these spaces require materials and direction to complete. Whether it's sourcing tile or textiles, carpet or paint, all of the information and guiding inspiration that I have gathered is used as a set of rules for the project. I am not above making a total mess of the studio during this time, but the rules we have established for each particular project help me here. They allow me to weed out extravagances or things that don't align with the clients' wants or needs—we are, after all, client focused. I say this, because, while there is certainly a thread of

OPPOSITE AND RIGHT: Collections from travels, memories from friends, and books are the real warmth in any space. They take the beautiful and make it personal.

my professional design aesthetic in each home, every interior is truly client driven. This allows me to individualize each space appropriate to the clients' own vernacular of reference and sense memory. I am not here to regurgitate the same style over and over, and hopefully our portfolio shows that dexterity. Of course,

we also must take into consideration the architecture (existing or to be realized) and function for the families who will live in the home. Function and comfort must coexist peacefully with each client's reference and sense memory.

OPPOSITE LEFT: The caning pattern in this coffee table by Charlotte Perriand is mimicked in the Turkish carpet underneath it.

OPPOSITE RIGHT: Rooms are very rarely made for standard size rugs. We often have simple workhorse rugs cut to the size of the room and float vintage rugs atop them for visual interest.

ABOVE: A few of the client's treasured pieces from many years of travel make this corner sing.

ABOVE: We never forget scent as a secret
ingredient to a finished room.

OPPOSITE: The client's antique carpet designed
this room for us. A saturated blue-and-ochre grass
cloth with navy wool drapes surround a vintage
burl dining table I bought at auction. Some of my
favorite dining chairs sport green leather for levity.

WINDERMERE

I was moved to write this section after receiving a text from the husband in this home: "My favorite room is still the media room, but on a winter's night the living room is fantastic." I don't get to see all of my clients all of the time—they are living their lives and I am letting them enjoy their homes—but when I get messages such as this one, it makes all of the hard (and not always so enjoyable) work worth it.

The clients bought this home with the intention of doing a major remodel and expansion in a wonderful old neighborhood in Seattle called Windermere. Calling this a remodel isn't quite fair as it is essentially an entirely new home. I was brought in at the beginning of the process to collaborate in tandem with the wonderfully talented and organized team at J.A.S. Design Build. We all worked together to create what I will call a contemporary English modern farmhouse. I had to make up this term, as the modern farmhouse label to me was starting to be played out. I wanted to warm it up and add a bit more detail to the oft-used vernacular.

Instead of white paint throughout we opted for warmer whites with slightly darker trim to create good shadows. The palette, unsurprisingly, came from the nature surrounding the house: a mix of warm neutrals, greens, blues, and every shade the sky can conjure up. I also had the joy of working with local galleries to start an art collection for the family, a process very different than interior design. You don't select a painting the way you select a chair—or at least I don't. The process for choosing displayed art is quite different and I like that we separate it. Visual art arrests a person in a different way than a great piece of furniture might. While I am not saying selecting furniture and lighting isn't emotional for some, art truly is (and should be) emotional for everyone. The objective isn't simply to fill wall space—it's a decision to invest in and live with an artist's point of view (or sometimes your own perceptions and interpretations of a piece). When building your own art collection, find pieces that resonate with you, considering how the work connects to your own reference and sense memory. Ask yourself what emotional response the art elicits in you.

At this point in my career, I regard this home as the closest thing to "our look," which is quite weird to say since it's the result of so many peoples' interests, opinions, and histories, but it just worked out that way. The mix of old and new, the color palette, the finishes, the art . . . all of it just felt right to me as it unfolded. It represents the family that lives here, and it holds up to three kids, one large dog, and a cat while still feeling sophisticated in that laid-back, Seattle kind of way. I very much look forward to seeing this home age over time and evolve with its inhabitants.

OPPOSITE AND ABOVE: We tend to keep the color story continuous (in one way or another) from room to room, making the home feel more harmonious but never boring. Here the green of the ceramic lamps in the dining room is continued in the entry with a pale-green console. The custom lampshades are a nod to traditional design.

We upholstered the walls in this TV room with a pale-green grass cloth and made the seating extra deep and comfortable for rainy days spent inside.

ABOVE: The architect on this project added interior windows (termed "re-lights") throughout this project allowing separation but also extending the light quality.

OPPOSITE: I firmly believe that counter seating should be as comfortable as the sofa in the your living room. These leather stools are not only functional for working in the kitchen but are also easy to clean.

ABOVE LEFT: Multiple lighting sources in a bedroom allow for many moods and functions.

ABOVE RIGHT: We placed this chaise near the window with the best views of the water: a place to read before bed or to enjoy a morning cup of coffee.

OPPOSITE: Classic materials and a balance of cool and warm make this primary bathroom luxurious.

BELLTOWN

Leaving behind a large family home in a residential neighborhood and moving into a much smaller downtown Seattle condo is a big step for anyone when considering how this new life will be led. This couple, who had raised and sent off the last of their children, decided to start the next chapter of their lives very differently. Their former home was fairly traditional with a classic floor plan. Their new home was fresh, contemporary, and open, with views of the Puget Sound on two sides.

They chose to start from scratch and craft a new, unexplored aesthetic in their condo. The wife spoke of always having wanted to live in a SoHo-esque loft with painted brick, exposed pipes, and a collection of items from all time periods and styles. The goal here became to mix styles, keep the palette neutral but warm, and add as much texture to the space as possible to take the slickness down a notch. Open floor plans can be very intimidating and we wanted to make sure to include all of the function of a traditional family home with clear room distinctions and welcoming seating plans in this new space. Rounded edges, incredibly textural and comfortable upholstery, and sculptural lighting was used to do just this. We took a slightly different path in the master bedroom by going just a tad darker, using neutral tones to create a moody retreat from the noise down below. In the extra bedroom–turned-study, we designed a custom desk, bookshelf, and daybed, with storage for daily use as an office and overflow storage for when guests come to stay. We treated this space differently, keeping a limited but bold palette of gray paint, black-and-cream ceruse wood, and gray wool fabrics. The result relates in approach to the rest of the home but enjoys a departure in palette. This project has become a calling card for my work—as it has been published many times and is noted quite often by my peers—and I am more than fine with that. It was so invigorating to work on a brand-new space with clients who trusted me and our shared vision. We agreed from the start to let the view be the champion here. Nature wins.

OPPOSITE AND ABOVE: Open floor plans can be just as challenging as small rooms. We placed this vintage console table with a lamp on top of it behind the sofa to softly delineate itself from the dining room in a similar color palette. The window sheers and materials tie the two spaces together and the custom dining table helps break down the apartment's hard lines.

The living room's sectional and swivel chair serve double duty here, allowing views of either the television or the Puget Sound in the distance.

OPPOSITE LEFT: I favor weaves over prints in most of my work; it not only offers a pattern to enjoy but also a surface texture to feel.

OPPOSITE RIGHT: A performance fabric covers the custom sectional for ease of cleaning and is balanced with cashmere bouclé in the pillows for extra comfort.

ABOVE: While I love fully upholstered seating the most for its comfort, a sculptural chair that allows you to see beyond itself can help a tight space and give visual interest as well.

OPPOSITE: A custom entry console, leather-wrapped mirror, and handmade lighting ensure that even the seemingly mundane spaces in a small apartment are part of the experience of a well-considered space.

ABOVE: I love good wall-to-wall carpet in a bedroom for its feel underfoot on cold mornings. We had the bedside table made to match the wall color we chose, and the draperies match the bed to add calm.

We outfitted this den with a custom-made desk, bookshelf, and daybed in a matching black-and-cream cerused finish for drama. We took our cues from cruise ship interiors to make the most of a small but mighty space. The glow of brass in the hardware and lighting balance the otherwise dark palette.

FIREHOUSE

This apartment, in the middle of Capitol Hill in Seattle, was formerly a firehouse but was split up into individual homes many years ago. Upon first entering the space during our initial interview, I knew I needed to do anything to get this job. The brick, the large black-trimmed windows, the ceilings, and the open floor plan were my late '90s, New York City, Thomas O'Brien dreams come true. By the time we had sat down to discuss the work ahead, I had already designed the entire place in my mind.

The client, who travels back and forth between Seattle and Los Angeles for work, had owned the apartment for a few years but, like most people with his packed schedule, hadn't tackled making it into a home. He didn't want endless meetings or back-and-forth phone calls to get the job done and, after reviewing a few mood boards, he entrusted us to the job. I should stress: this is not the norm, and quite honestly, it's a very stressful approach. As much as you might think it would be a dream for a designer like me (who loves to talk about the organic nature of the design process), it's not. There are technical elements of my job, such as spreadsheets and sign-offs on specific pieces, that make me happier than you could imagine. I like the order that comes with the business side of my creative chaos (especially when so much of what we create is custom and therefore not returnable). Well, I needed to get over the lack of structure and just get to the task at hand. I didn't stray from my version of the late '90s New York City loft. I couldn't do much wrong with these architectural bones—we didn't even paint downstairs except for the kitchen. We kept the palette neutral, comfortable, and created multiple seating areas on the main floor for entertaining, which our client does quite a bit when he is in town. Upstairs are two bedrooms, two bathrooms, and an outdoor patio—all of which posed a challenge, being, in fact, New York City size. When spaces are small, I tend to embrace their diminutive nature and make them super cozy. We carpeted the whole floor in a gray wool and matched the walls, trim, and ceiling in a complementary gray paint to minimize the small footprint and eaves in the space. It should be noted that this project is included in this book because the client loved it all. I am hoping to get down to his LA home next to see if he lets me loose again.

OPPOSITE: We imagined a casual seating area right next to the dining room for pre-dinner cocktails and conversation.

ABOVE: An artful arrangement in the entry also allows for key and mail storage; the ottoman provides a place to sit when putting on shoes.

We treated this large entry space like a gallery, opting for a vintage cupboard for coats (instead of a built-in closet) and a center table, which allows the area to function as a breakfast room.

ABOVE LEFT: A very small, primary bedroom with hard eaves called for a dark and sultry palette.

ABOVE RIGHT: Custom bedside tables and multiple lighting sources were a must for this tight space.

OPPOSITE: The office is just off the primary bedroom, holding a dresser for closet overflow and offering another space to relax.

ABOVE: In the kitchen, we chose a brick-red backsplash to complement the brick throughout the loft.

OPPOSITE: The patio off the office has sliding doors that bring the outside in, even in the middle of the city.

MERCER ISLAND

I met this client through mutual friends a few years prior to working on the home featured here. She had invited us to her existing home for our firm to design a living room, dining room, entry, and master suite. She was thrilled with our plans and gave us the green light to begin producing everything. Then, unexpectedly, she called to say that she had put her house on the market and was moving into the rental of her dreams in a completely different neighborhood. We are nothing as a design firm if we aren't flexible: we reviewed what was already in production, tweaked some items, and added new things for the rental, which she and her daughters enjoyed for a spell. When our client and her partner purchased a spec home halfway through construction, they brought me on board immediately to select the finishes, plumbing, lighting, tile, and flooring—and to make, what would have already been a lovely home, truly theirs. The family has a fondness for Mexico, handmade textures, and comfort. Taking this into consideration, we designed this third home with a neutral but warm palette that would support their busy lifestyle and create a sense of ease at the end of a long day. We used all of the pieces from the previous rental home in guest bedrooms and upstairs TV room, then created new pieces for the main living spaces. I think the master bedroom, with its four-poster bed, grass cloth walls, and a mix of wonderful textiles, is my favorite room. It is pure comfort and gets wonderful light. The downstairs open kitchen, dining, and living room were not easy to design as I wanted each room to have similar but notable identities. We ended up using one defined palette and explored shapes and scale from there. The client trusted me from day one, regardless of her already impeccable taste, and that was a tremendous compliment. The achieved goal for the home was ease, intimacy, and a place to be enjoyed by all. Sometimes, the third try really is the charm.

ABOVE: The light quality in this living room was the major player. Multiple periods of furniture enhance the collected feel.

OPPOSITE: A look into the office. The art by Bradley Duncan gives a cue of color to come from that more saturated space.

OPPOSITE: We designed custom cabinetry for the office and lacquered it in a green-blue shade that picks up on one of the client's favorite textiles in the adjacent room, visually connecting the two very different spaces.

RIGHT: The powder room was inspired by the client's favorite hotel in Mexico and features a custom marble sink, brass-and-alabaster sconces for its light quality, and a wallpaper by Laura Aviva.

OPPOSITE: In the dining room a reclaimed oak table is balanced by black oak-and-leather chairs and a contemporary light fixture.

ABOVE: A planter by Bari Ziperstein and mirror by Ben and Aja Blanc allow the entry to be not only functional but also artful.

ABOVE: We selected slabs of calacatta gold for the counters and backsplash to keep the materials to a minimum there.

OPPOSITE: Classic New England-style chairs from Rhode Island at the heads of the table add another line to the dining room.

A four-poster bed in two wood finishes, patterned grass cloth, and a textural palette make this primary bedroom warm and inviting. The day bed is from our furniture collection and is covered in a cashmere bouclé. The tramp art frame and vintage photographs were bought at auction.

OPPOSITE: Balancing textures can be tricky: you need solid, small-scale, medium-scale, and large-scale textures to pull it off, while being conscious of color weights as well.

ABOVE: Bedside tables in a green lacquer offset all of the matte textures.

ABOVE: Indoor-outdoor living was very important to this client. We used a darker but similar palette of materials to tie the two spaces together.

OPPOSITE: Add an outdoor rug and generous seating along with good heating elements to ensure you can use an outdoor space all year long.

YARROW POINT

Sometimes, at the end of the day, interior design is just a service I provide and the relationship between client and designer ends at the invoice. This project, situated on the water in Yarrow Point, a small enclave near Bellevue on the east side, was not that. I remember taking the scheduled call from my bed early on a Saturday morning and connecting with the client immediately: she was in her early thirties and, after a number of years in the Bay Area, was moving back to Seattle where she had grown up. She had purchased a midcentury home and wanted to mark this transitional stage in her life with a remodel of not only the home, but herself. Little did I know, she would help me realize that I, too, needed a life remodel.

Our goal for the home was to honor the architecture but strip away the dated additions from the '80s and '90s that did not suit my client's aesthetic. She asked me to push her into a more colorful palette for the house and, while I don't consider myself a super colorful designer, I obliged in my own earthy way. Well, the colorful-palette exercise turned out to be just that—an exercise. Halfway through the first presentation, we agreed to strip away most of the color and instead landed on a palette that reflected the landscapes my client discovered on her many travels to South Africa and the colors of nature surrounding her new home. The furniture was selected for maximum comfort with a mix of contemporary lines, textured one-offs, and nods to her love of San Francisco traditional design. We talked at length about light quality, "finding our north star," poodles, and unpacked some tough personal things over many design-turned–emotional purge meetings. I remember most my drives back home or to the office after leaving her home. I would usually jot down some advice she had given me during our chat or look up a book she had suggested or just cry a good cry. She was a true design champion for me: She listened. She trusted. Her additions to our ideas made the home truly hers, a place where she could heal, reconnect with family, discover a new path, and just be. I can't thank her enough for the job but, more importantly, for the time and words she gifted me. The biggest lesson I learned during our time together was to not hold on to those words, but to share them with the next person who needed to hear them and heal.

A vintage Moroccan rug and multiple types of seating make this area off the kitchen very inviting and add softness to the space. The photograph was purchased at the Seattle Art Fair.

OPPOSITE: One of my favorite light fixtures for its timeless look and light quality floats over a reclaimed oak dining table with a set of contemporary dining chairs and vintage Oushak rug.

ABOVE: The all-white kitchen ensures the space stays bright during the long, dark winters.

LEFT: In the primary bedroom, a cool palette of soft blues and beige is calming and restful. A vintage desk topped with new marble is now used as a vanity.

OPPOSITE: Grass cloth is always a good idea for a bedroom, in my opinion. The bed's extended arms feel as if it's giving you a hug.

WHIDBEY ISLAND

This home, located in a private area of Whidbey Island, has been the summer home to two generations now. My client, who lives in New York but grew up in Seattle, wished to revitalize the beloved property. She had grown up visiting the Whidbey Island house every summer, an experience she wanted for her own children—for them to forge a stronger connection to their West Coast family roots. This project was quite a departure in color and style from my usual work, but inspiration sprang from my childhood in Newport, Rhode Island. The client trusted that, despite my portfolio of neutrals, I could execute her dreams of a red, white, and blue home, replete with ticking fabric as a tribute to the home's past.

This house was a delight to design, and the process flowed from my fingers more naturally than anything I had worked on for years at that point. The universe had sent me what I needed at the right time. I channeled my favorite rooms from designers such as Markham Roberts and Ashley Whittaker—whom I have the utmost respect for, and for whom I would gladly retrieve either of their coffees, any day—to establish the right seaside ethos for the home's décor.

We stripped away a remodel, which had been done in the early '90s and hadn't aged well, by redoing the kitchen and all the baths. We installed new flooring, trim, lighting, a fireplace, and windows, and finished up with fresh coats of paint. When it came time to furnish, I practically had to start over in regards to textiles. Red is, in fact, my least favorite color, but navy blue is my favorite, so on we charged. As the home was coming together I realized it wasn't so far from our firm's regular oeuvre: it was my interpretation of something that has been done for decades—the classic summer house—in a new setting. I layered in existing rugs, primitive art, and side tables that had been left behind to give the space a little age. The boys' room is a reference to a room that designer Meg Braff did for her boys in Newport, Rhode Island, back in 2006. For ours, I incorporated some tweaks, such as the custom gray-blue ceruse dresser, which we adapted from my furniture line with Lawson-Fenning.

I love visiting this home (taking the ferry from Seattle instantly takes ten points off my blood pressure): just pausing for a bit, smelling the sea air, driving the long winding roads to the house, feeling the crunch of sand under my feet, and relishing sunsets from the front porch . . . it doesn't get much better. I love that this project came into my life when it did. It was meaningful for me to get back to some of my roots in design, feeling a bit like I was designing back in Newport, Rhode Island, hopefully impressing my former boss. I am forever grateful for that nostalgic glimpse.

OPPOSITE AND ABOVE: Red, white, and blue and a layering of multiple patterns over more traditional furniture lines in the living room, along with a collection of auction finds from varying periods, help make this home feel found and less decorated. We redesigned the fireplace with more classic empire details where it had originally been an entire wall of dark river rock.

ABOVE: This is a summer house and the indoor-outdoor connection was paramount for maximum enjoyment.

OPPOSITE: Small and large ticking stripes were used generously throughout the home as a reference to the owner's childhood.

OPPOSITE: Pattern on pattern, from the ticking stripes on the ottomans and drapes to the custom lampshades, and a selection of contemporary and vintage art.

ABOVE LEFT: An awkward area in the eaves of the top floor is filled with found treasures and becomes a place to rest.

ABOVE RIGHT: The pop of a red lacquer lampshade makes this vignette lively.

OPPOSITE: A plaid sofa, navy blue grass cloth, and a collection of vintage tortoise shells make for a cozy den.

ABOVE: The boys' room is a nod to Meg Braff's boys' room in Newport where I grew up, and features a custom dresser from my furniture collection in a cerused blue finish.

LEFT: The primary bathroom's cabinetry is painted the same atmospheric green as the bedroom. With Carrara tiles and a vintage claw-foot tub, this space will never go out of style.

OPPOSITE: In the primary bedroom, we connected two queen-size beds by having a custom headboard made to span the length of the wall and used the same silk-and-linen pattern for the bedskirts. The soft green paint was pulled from the vines in the print and is balanced by the ikat print in the bed roll and the large stripe of the dhurrie rug.

SAN FRANCISCO

This classic San Francisco Victorian home is the second home I have done for this particular client. Both homes, which share a similar clean and masculine aesthetic, have been about beginning new chapters in life. When we met to work on his first place, he had just gone through a tough breakup and wanted to wipe the slate clean of the home he had previously shared with his ex. This client travels a lot for work so both homes needed to be comfortable, and the design process needed to be straightforward and completed fairly quickly. When we met, we discovered our mutual love for large-scale minimalist paintings and he had a great collection to work from. After the first meeting, he trusted me implicitly.

While I loved the results of his Seattle home, I was thrilled for his move to San Francisco and his opportunity to create a true home for himself—not to mention, the bones of the classic Victorian house he chose could make any décor look good. With the floors and kitchen in good order we set about painting the whole place (including the doors, which were many), changing out hardware and lighting, and furnishing the place for this new chapter in life. We took into consideration his large-scale art, which now had more space to breathe, and pulled colors from them into the rooms' furnishings. While this client is often quite reserved, he has confided to me on several occasions what this process has done for him in terms of moving on and aiming higher; the pleasures of a comfortable space to return to after extensive travels; and how proud he is to entertain his friends here when he is in town. As I am writing this, he is considering a move to New York and has already sent me listings for homes he is considering. He is wholly untethered as to what his next chapter could be; he embodies adventure. His homes have, and will always be, a place of respite to return to—a true luxury.

OPPOSITE: The original marble fireplace in the living room juxtaposed with a photograph by Rafael Soldi and ceramics by Mirena Kim.

ABOVE: A view from the dining room into the slim living room.

OPPOSITE AND RIGHT: We had all of the interior doors painted black and added brass center knobs to evoke a Parisian feel in all the rooms. The ceiling fixture takes advantage of the ceiling height and, along with the furnishings, adds a contemporary counterpoint to the home's age.

ABOVE: A tufted bed in gray linen creates a calm feeling in the primary bedroom that sits in the back of the home, receiving the most muted afternoon light.

OPPOSITE: An articulating lamp mounted to the wall doesn't disturb the lines of the windows above.

CHELAN

About three and half hours east of Seattle is a town named Chelan. A well-known summer destination for many Pacific Northwest families, it has a large lake for boating and swimming. In the winter, it is quiet and calm and lovely with its 360-degree mountain views, and winter is the only time I have actually spent there. I like these types of getaway retreats regardless of the intended use because they take its inhabitants out of their everyday mentality and, design wise, I can be a little more experimental. The family, whom I have known for more than eight years and who now have three young children, desired a great winter escape in a planned community without it looking like a planned-community home.

The family's Seattle home is very traditional in style—not stuffy by any means, but appropriate for the bones of the space. They wanted something very different for this second home, inspired by a cleaner, Scandinavian look, and wanted a muted palette to go along with it. We worked with the existing architectural plans for the home but selected all new finishes including floors, paint, tile, plumbing, and lighting—as well as a new layout for the kitchen to make it much more custom than the original plans called for, and to suit their needs and aesthetic goals better. We then went about furnishing the home with kid-friendly but stylish furniture and art. This home needed to hold up to snowy boots, movie nights, and many guests. Materials were chosen for their durability and multifunction. Pops of true white throughout the house speak to the snowtipped mountains, but the overall feel is warmth; it keeps this family coming back even more often than they thought they would.

The dining room looking into the kitchen, a very heavily used space by a large family, features walnut and black oak and a rug to delineate spaces. The kitchen's pale green cabinetry is a nod to seagrass.

OPPOSITE: The textures in the rug and pottery reference the snow-dappled mountains that surround the home.

ABOVE: A guest room is full of all the same comforts as the main bedroom.

LEFT: In the main bath, warm and cool are balanced with sage green cabinetry, leather mirrors, and brass and bronze accents.

OPPOSITE: In the primary suite, we kept the color scheme of the rest of the home consistent: a walnut mirror and brass accent lighting helps balance the cool tones. Because this family uses the home primarily as a wintertime retreat, we kept the palette geared toward cozy winter days spent inside with a good book.

MAGNOLIA

This house is located in a storybook part of Seattle called Magnolia: a place where there is essentially one bridge in and one bridge out, you know all your neighbors, and the views of the Sound are priceless. I love the age and scale of many of the homes built in this neighborhood throughout the 1950s and 1960s, though this was *not* one of those homes. This new-construction house belongs to dear friends of another client of mine who also lives in Magnolia. These couples have larger-than-life personalities, throw spectacular parties, and have a zest for life that is rarely seen in other people. I was brought in early on in the building process to select or confirm the finishes and layout of the home, and then to furnish accordingly. The inspiration for the home's interiors was equal parts Pacific Northwest and Palm Springs, although the clients tended to favor the Palm Springs references much more. I had to be careful here: Seattle is not Palm Springs and vice versa. Forcing an aesthetic into a home with so many windows (where nature automatically becomes a big part of the aesthetic inside) can be tricky. While many of the lines of the furniture are very midcentury, or things you may find in a Palm Springs home, the color palette needed to stay true to nature in Seattle and be warm enough for the long winters here. The walnut ceiling paneling in the entry and dining room helps cast a warm and cozy feeling in those areas of the home, and the stone used for the fireplace adds some great texture. The master bedroom is my favorite room (as it often is), with a palette built on natural neutrals that are soothing yet not boring. There are nods to midcentury design in the custom bed and nightstands, which were based on designs from the 1970s. The entry also featured the prototype for what would be called the George daybed from my furniture collection with Lawson-Fenning, named after my dachshund. Overall, our goal was to create a home that reflected the age and character of other homes in Magnolia, while combining a midcentury-modern aesthetic that reflected its homeowners' zest for life. I think we succeeded.

ABOVE: Stone, linen, terrazzo, and the
bleached manzanita branch illustrate the
home's ethos in one small corner.

OPPOSITE: The walnut-clad bar and
lowered counter seating in the kitchen
serve as a place for casual daily life.

A mix of wool, bouclé, hemp, jute, lacquered linen, leather, wood, and glass makes this living room complex in palette but easy on the eyes.

Looking outside through the wall of bifold doors, you understand the clients' affinity for the view and the nature we value so much in the Pacific Northwest. The silk rug softens the terrazzo floors.

ABOVE: Midcentury classics—a custom live-edge dining table and floating walnut shelf, both made in Seattle—are paired with silk wallcovering and a painting by Michael Duryea made out of coffee grounds and paint.

OPPOSITE: The George daybed from our furniture collection is covered in a textural bouclé fabric, while the oversize mirror balances the light in the entry.

OPPOSITE: The custom bed wears a linen velvet and is paired with custom walnut bedside tables, a brass-legged tufted ottoman, linen draperies, a hemp-and-silk rug, and a custom light fixture that throws light toward the ceiling.

ABOVE: A vintage Zanuso chair in the corner of the bedroom and the Aquidneck Chest from our collection greets you as you enter the suite.

ABOVE: I tend to match the walls, upholstery, and carpet in media rooms to keep it relaxed and easy.

OPPOSITE: The primary bathroom is covered in travertine and features a simplified version of a midcentury floating vanity.

VICTORIA

This penthouse apartment, right on the water in downtown Victoria, British Columbia, was purchased as a city getaway for a long-time client, and (truth be told) I didn't actually set foot in this apartment until installation day. We designed the entire thing from Seattle while it was being completed, working with scaled floor plans and photos of the space through the seasons and in different light qualities. This being the penthouse, the views and the curves of the architecture in the main living space would guide many of my design choices. The client gave me carte blanche to imagine a sleek but layered and textured place for him and his friends to crash after a night on the town. The other homes of his that we have done are old, dark, and dramatic spaces demanding large-scale pieces, which juxtapose with his incredible rock-and-roll photography collection. This space was to be different: it's about open and bright spaces that allow for entertaining and ease. The palette of stone, cream, cerused woods, black marble, plaster, and ash carries throughout the two-bedroom apartment and is accented by jolts of golden rod, cranberry, ocean blue, and weaves. I often favor weaves over patterns as they not only open much for interpretation but they don't age as quickly as pattern design and offer great surface texture your body can experience as well. The night lights from the boats in the water and the sunset just beyond the windows on an early fall night are remarkable in this space and give so much depth to what may first appear as just bare white walls. When I think of this home I hear the sounds of the band My Bloody Valentine and smell hinoki wood on a crisp fall morning.

Curved lines in the furniture play to the architecture in the main living space, which does double duty as living and dining. We mixed wood tones and species throughout the pieces to create visual interest.

OPPOSITE: The suede sofa will age like a great pair of shoes and is paired with interesting textures in the same tones.

ABOVE: The vintage Mazandaran rug adds color to an otherwise beige-and-black color story and references the water view.

LEFT AND OPPOSITE: Swivel chairs are one of my greatest not-so-secret weapons in design. A clean design that can be taken in any stylistic direction based on upholstery choice, they help open-plan rooms work harder and allow for both view gazing and socializing. I make mine a little larger so you can wrap your legs up in them.

ABOVE: Balancing weights of furniture is important in any space: pieces that ground the room and pieces that feel light and can be seen through.

OPPOSITE: The veining in the marble-topped table is referenced in the structured weave on the dining chairs.

ABOVE: In the entry, a custom plaster console table mimics the texture of the walls and holds the ephemera of a well-traveled life.

OPPOSITE: A look into the primary bedroom from the entry hall and a stack of the client's vast collection of original punk photos.

OPPOSITE AND RIGHT: We
added a custom dresser to
balance concrete and oak in the
bedroom. The chair is by Stephen
Kenn and can be used inside
or outside. The pillow is made
from vintage Japanese textiles.

GIUSEPPE PENONE

ABOVE: The bed features a horizontal stripe to broaden the small footprint of the room with custom nightstands tucked in on either side.

OPPOSITE: A bench covered in a deconstructed plaid wool pairs with greens and cranberry to add some unexpected color.

GIUSEPPE PENONE   GAGOSIAN GALLERY

OUTRO

This is not the end. There is no end to creativity and expression. Every home is in a state of constant evolution and should be embraced as such. At the end of a large installation, there is always a strange moment when the clients think everything is finished—that the changes and improvements that have been put into place are the be-all and end-all of their design journey. That couldn't be further from the truth. I will no doubt see these projects evolve in the years to come, just as you will see your own space evolve over time. Change is not something to fear but something to embrace. It doesn't mean the original work has been a failure, rather, the work represents one chapter. Move this here, swap the living room lamps for the master bedroom lamps, rearrange your bookshelf, and on and on. The energy that surrounds these objects in our lives is best kept in motion. I encourage everyone to challenge their notion of permanence and instead go with the flow.

Before buying our first home, I had lived in ten different apartments in ten years—some for only six months! Now this nomadic way of life isn't for everyone, but with every move I felt joy and excitement in the possibilities of reusing my long-loved pieces in each new place, selling what no longer served me, and picking up newly discovered objects along the way. The new walls I had to explore always inspired and challenged me. Each move was an opportunity that allowed me to express myself and try things out. I once "wallpapered" a dining room in xerox copies of black-and-white botanical studies with wheat paste and shellac. I have painted a bathroom high-gloss black, changed every light fixture, made my own drapery rods, stripped floors, and conducted countless other experiments. My poor landlords! But a scrappy kid is a scrappy kid. Whatever your situation is, whether you're living in a rental or your forever home, make your space something that supports you and something you support. The energy goes both ways.

SOURCES

FURNITURE

Lawson-Fenning
Los Angeles, CA
www.lawsonfenning.com

Nickey Kehoe
Los Angeles, CA
www.nickeykehoe.com

Harbinger
Los Angeles, CA
www.harbingerLA.com

Made Goods
City of Industry, CA
www.madegoods.com

Hollywood at Home
Los Angeles, CA
www.hollywoodathome.com

Bunny Williams Home
New York, NY
www.bunnywilliamshome.com

Grain Design
Bainbridge Island, WA
www.graindesign.com

HM Duke Design
Seattle, WA
www.hmdukedesign.com

Egg Collective
New York, NY
www.eggcollective.com

O&G Studio
Warren, RI
www.oandgstudio.com

Casamidy
San Miguel de Allende, Mexico
www.casamidy.com

TEXTILES

Romo
www.romo.com

Zak+Fox
www.zakandfox.com

Phillip Jeffries
www.phillipjeffries.com

Stark
www.starkcarpet.com

Glant Textiles
www.glant.com

Samuel & Sons
www.samuelandsons.com

Chelsea Textiles
www.chelseatextiles.com

Studio Four NYC
www.studiofournyc.com

L'Aviva Home
www.lavivahome.com

Clarence House
www.clarencehouse.com

Kravet
www.kravet.com

Moore & Giles
www.mooreandgiles.com

Holland & Sherry
www.hollandandsherry.com

Armadillo
www.armadillo-co.com

LIGHTING

Visual Comfort
Houston, TX
www.visualcomfort.com

Apparatus
Los Angeles, CA / New York, NY
www.apparatusstudio.com

Workstead
Brooklyn, NY
www.workstead.com

Vaughan Designs
New York, NY, and other locations
www.vaughandesigns.com

Lindsey Adelman
Los Angeles, CA / New York, NY
www.lindseyadelman.com

The Urban Electric Co.
North Charleston, SC
www.urbanelectric.com

Stone and Sawyer
Delhi, NY
www.stoneandsawyer.com

SHOPS AND SHOWROOMS

Hedgerow
Edison, WA
www.hedgerowedison.com

Housewright
Seattle, WA
www.housewrightgallery.com

Maison Luxe
Seattle, WA
www.maisonluxe.net

Inform Interiors
Vancouver, British Columbia
www.informinteriors.com

The Future Perfect
Los Angeles + San Francisco, CA /
New York, NY
www.thefutureperfect.com

The Dixon Group
Seattle, WA
www.thedixongroup.net

Trammell-Gagné
Seattle, WA
www.tgshowroom.com

Kelly Forslund
Seattle, WA
www.kellyforslund.com

Jennifer West
Seattle, WA
www.jwshowroom.com

Driscoll Robbins Fine Carpets
Seattle, WA
www.driscollrobbins.com

Susan Wheeler Home
Seattle, WA
www.susanwheelerhome.com

Red Ticking
Seattle, WA
www.redticking.com

**Newport Lamp & Shade
Company**
Newport, RI
www.newportlampandshade.com

Garde
Los Angeles, CA
www.gardeshop.com

March
San Francisco, CA
www.marchsf.com

PAINT

Farrow and Ball
www.farrow-ball.com

INSTALLATION

Express Installation Services
Seattle, WA
www.eisseattle.com

Fanis Beroukas
Wallpaper hanging

ARTISTS AND GALLERIES

M Quan
www.mquan.com

Winston Wächter
www.seattle.winstonwachter.com

Lakshmi Muirhead
www.lakshmimuirhead.com

Victoria Morris
www.victoriamorrispottery.com

Mirena Kim
www.mirenakim.com

Bari Ziperstein
www.bariziperstein.com

Ben Medansky
www.benmedansky.com

Linda Hodges Gallery
www.lindahodgesgallery.com

Seattle Art Source
www.seattleartsource.com

With a background in painting and conceptual art, Brian Paquette brings a singular point of view to the interior design scene. Rather than follow a particular style, he draws inspiration from a variety of sources: architecture, travel, and the natural world, to name a few. For Brian, interior design is not something sterile or static; it's a living extension of art, meant to be touched, used, and admired. That mindset is at the heart of Brian Paquette Interiors.